Witnessing Ted

THE JOURNEY TO POTENTIAL
THROUGH GRIEF AND LOSS

Diane,

May your healing path
connect with warmth
and love.

Blessi

Carol Poteat with **Ted Wiard, LPCC, CGC**

ISBN: 1461046122
ISBN-13: 9781461046127
Library of Congress Control Number: 2011905506

This book is for all who have suffered from loss.
May you be heard and may you witness.

Table of Contents

Introduction: *El Descanso*

As Spanish Franciscan missionaries made their way into northern New Mexico, they intermittently took sanctuary in stopping places for rest and recovery. These *descansos*, literally translated as "resting places", held them, allowing them to return to their daily rituals, tend to their spiritual and physical needs, and connect with others to share their stories. After a time at the *descanso*, they continued with their travels until they reached another and it was time to rest again.

The word *descanso* now signifies the roadside memorials along highways. Usually represented with crosses, they mark the places where loved ones have died in a tragic accident.

Just as the word has shifted in meaning, so has the importance of how our culture views the recovery time of grief and loss. We have been taught to shy away from the pain, stoically intellectualizing it, and numbing our emotions until circumstances force us to address it.

On my journey, I find a *descanso* in the original sense of the word. Golden Willow Retreat, founded by Ted and Marcella Wiard, is one of the few sanctuaries in the United States dedicated to helping people with the emotional healing process from loss. Golden Willow clients are given the time to rest and nourish themselves, the tools to glean wisdom from their grief, and the space to connect to the higher power of their understanding before they continue on their journey.

It is here that I am held to rest and to hear Ted's story. It is here that I am heard when sharing some of my own story. Woven among my day to day rituals, it is here that I learn to accept and bestow the permission to grieve and to heal.

In *Witnessing Ted*, each chapter begins with a snapshot of Ted's emotional journey through grief. We then return to the present, where the process of grief unfolds through my understanding of Ted's teachings.

This book serves to help those who have suffered and live with loss, not only through death but in the countless life events that shake our foundation of reality. Thus, it is for everyone, and it is written so that we may better understand what is necessary to our healing process. With that understanding, we accept permission to seek our own personal *descansos* along the way and open ourselves to a life more aligned to our true potential.

Along the journey, we discover hope.

Cuando se pierde la esperanza, se pierde todo. (When hope is lost, all is lost.)

Loss is a shaking, cracking, or shattering of the foundation of our personal reality, at times subtle and at other times, extreme.

The Fourth Cross

Fall of 1996 - Taos, New Mexico

The pickup came to a stop on the shoulder of the highway. The door opened and dusty boots made their way to the truck's bed. Ian turned and paused while reading the names on the three tiny crosses of the descanso nestled in the hill: Keri Wiard, Amy Wiard, and Rachel Devlin, all lost in a collision with a garbage truck.

The accident had rocked the small community of Taos. Within five years time, Ian's friend Ted had lost his brother, Richard, in a fishing accident, his wife, Leslie, to cancer, and then his daughters, ages six and nine, along with their maternal grandmother. How could one man face such tremendous loss?

The thought took Ian back to his own near-fatal accident. While lying in a coma, he had heard Ted's voice urging him back to life. Now, his plea went out to Ted.

Ted had been a part of his life for as long as Ian could remember. Ted came to his dad's cabin on hunting trips and he was also his fifth grade teacher. Despite their age difference, Ted was a trusted friend, someone he could always count on. He had been gone for months now, travelling in Hawaii, New Zealand, and Australia, trying to make sense out of what made no sense. To him, Ted was just as gone as these girls.

With that thought, he lowered the truck bed in a clap of dust and tugged, shifting the weight of its contents to his brawny shoulders. He slowly made his way to the top of the hill where he erected the large wooden cross perpendicular to those below. This cross was for his friend. The Ted he had known had died.

What Are Loss and Grief?

I stepped into the crisp Albuquerque day to wait for my ride. I had missed my shuttle, but having surmised that my flight would be late, Ted was already half way there to pick me up. I wondered if I would be the same Carol upon my return.

I had flown here from Charlotte to learn about grief from loss through Ted's eyes. My intent was to write a book, with his help, that offered people hope as their healing process unfolded. Having known him for years, I was already familiar with Ted's story. We met at Terra Nova Center in the western mountains of North Carolina, studied together in the ministerial program, had been ordained together, and remained tied over the years through his marriage to my best friend, Marcella.

Little did I know that as I learned about grief, the door would open to my own. Over the next three days, I spent time with Ted and heard the grief process unfold through his story of loss. For hours on end, I listened as he revealed its psychological aspects, and through it all, my own grief surfaced, bringing more healing.

Ted's SUV pulled up to the curb. He bounded out to help with my bag, excitement pouring through his bright smile and blue eyes. We settled into the car and, after initial greetings, the lessons began. We wound our way toward a lunch stop in Santa Fe as I learned about loss and the grief process.

Ted explained that each time we suffer a loss, our perception of self dies as well. Loss is a shaking, cracking, or shattering of the foundation of our personal reality, at times subtle and at others, extreme. As loss is realized, the illusion of control is disturbed or distressed and the existing perception of self falls away.

Loss takes many forms throughout our lives. We feel loss as an ideal day fades to sunset and we lose those we love through estrangement and death. We may experience loss through an array of traumas: physical, sexual, mental, emotional, and spiritual. We lose our innocence and our sense of wonder. We lose ties to family and community. Friendships fade and fail. We lose trust to betrayal, theft, and abuse. Dreams go unattained. We lose our peace of mind.

We experience loss though divorce, breakups, and miscarriage. We lose our power, our drive, and our self-control. We lose the regard that others hold for us, and we lose regard for ourselves. We lose credibility and our sense of humor. As our children grow, we lose their need for us. We miss the experience of being a parent by not having them at all.

We lose opportunities, freedoms, promotions, and jobs. We lose savings, status, belongings, stability, and homes. We lose our health, our abilities, our memory, our beauty, our muscle, and our youth.

We don masks of who we think we should be, and we lose our authenticity. We lose our focus, our will power, our identity, our self, and our hope. We become numb to life, and we lose connection to ourselves and to others.

Our rites of passage carry elements of loss as well. Even happy occasions such as graduations, marriages, births, promotions, and retirement demand that we redefine ourselves, losing who we once were and stepping into a new self.

When loss shakes or shatters our perception of self, we experience the natural emotions of the grief process. We feel trapped in the past and fearful of the future. With no firm foundation to hold us, we go into a free fall where the past and the future collide, impeding our ability to be in the present. We are prone to grasp anything or anyone that can make the world feel more manageable.

These feelings of loss are often dismissed by self or others. We bury our feelings, telling ourselves that "it's not that big of a deal" or "I just won't think about it," which causes suppressed emotions to manifest as discomfort and dis-ease. Ted warned that many can live their lives in that state, choosing to close off their hearts and numb their emotions. They become like the "walking dead," flat and deaf to their pain, their joy, and their higher call to evolve.

When we allow ourselves to consciously engage in the grief process, we open to the process of personal transformation. We enter into our *descansos* of recovery, expression, and reconnection and are able to create a bridge to the next level of our journey. Through time and with grace, we accept our situation with new light and wisdom.

Grief is not the answer to a single event, but a lifelong endeavor. Through the patient expression of our losses, we continually redefine ourselves, becoming more and more aligned to our true self and our innate potential.

Conscious grieving is the ultimate rite of passage and unfolds throughout our time on earth. It is the answer to the universe's call for our highest level of service and growth.

Indeed, it is what we are all here to experience.

By expressing our feelings, we open the door
to hope by connecting to our hearts.

Mai Tai

Spring of 1998 - Tryon, North Carolina

"Brain tumors?" Ted exclaimed as he heard the diagnosis. "This can't be. No, no, not Mai Tai!"

The phone call seemed like a bad dream. Here he was, more than a thousand miles away in North Carolina, trying to get his life together, and Mai Tai was dying.

Leslie had given him the Golden Retriever-Black Lab mix for his birthday shortly after they were married. The lovable pup found his name when he tipped over Ted's drink and began lapping it up. Through the years, Mai Tai had come to embody unconditional love.

He accompanied Ted on mind-clearing walks during Leslie's battle with cancer. He was a tireless companion and guardian to the girls. Like a timeline for his life, Mai Tai had shared Ted's love and, later, his pain as Richard, Leslie, Keri, and Amy were taken from him. Mai Tai was the witness that helped shoulder Ted's sorrow and the glue that held him together.

The loss of Mai Tai sent Ted into free fall.

Our Emotional Boats

On our way to Golden Willow Retreat, Ted and I stopped at a local favorite in Santa Fe for a late lunch. Still on East Coast time, I was grateful for the break and relishing the idea of authentic New Mexico cuisine. I nibbled on a sopapilla drizzled with honey, while Ted sketched a boat on a paper napkin.

He shared an interesting metaphor. The human psyche is like a sail boat. The "boat" begins to take in water in the form of loss before our first breath.

For example, in the womb, the mother may be sick or involved in stressful situations. The fetus registers this loss of tranquility as a loss of safety and water is taken into the "hold". The baby experiences extreme contrast as it is delivered into a room that is cold and brightly lit. More water leaks into the "boat".

The baby learns that he can get what he wants if he cries. He cries for someone to hold him. He cries to be fed. He cries when he is wet. One day, his cries get no response, and his way of controlling his world isn't working anymore. He feels unsure and unsafe. More "water" comes aboard.

As a youngster, he experiences new and challenging environments. He is made fun of. He fails a test. He is punished. A friend moves away. A pet dies. He may suffer from or witness abuse. Perhaps his parents get divorced, a grandparent passes away, and he is moved to another state, leaving all he knows behind. More and more "water" comes in, sometimes drip by drip, sometimes by the bucket load.

By the time the boy finishes high school, a time when one is supposedly just embarking on life, his "boat" sits with tattered sails, low in the water, its hull already full.

Another loss comes along, but because the hull is full, no matter how "big" or "small" it may seem, the loss demands acknowledgment. This loss runs down the mast and reverberates into the hull, tickling all the boy's past losses, both expressed and unexpressed.

By consciously grieving this most recent loss, he unknowingly acknowledges all of his other losses. He is able to release "water" from the past, even though he isn't doing so consciously. The rebuff of the teacher, the girl who was standoffish, or not making the football team move through the "bilge pump" as the young man's perception of self evolves. These losses now become facts on his life timeline rather than emotionally charged truths and triggers that define and confine him.

Some losses do not go through the bilge pump and must be brought to the surface to be healed and transformed. This process has no timeline, but it is the true quest for healing. With no "shore" in sight, the young man must allow his emotions to ebb and flow on his journey.

As he is able, he seeks witness by expressing his emotions to himself and others. In doing so, he claims the permission to grieve and opens the door to hope by connecting, however slightly, to his heart. His expression requires compassion and acceptance as he seeks to be seen, heard, and valued through the telling and retelling of his story. Connected to his feelings, he "flows into his heart." His tears give him the focus of newer eyes, and the pieces of his shattered identity begin to be redefined and transformed into a wiser version of self.

As they listen to his story, the others in his life receive a benefit as well. They identify with the ripples of his story and relate it to their own, creating either a subconscious flow through their own bilge pumps or allowing a suppressed loss to register on their masts of consciousness for healing.

Because hearing another's story affects the water in our own "boats", we must be mindful *to witness*, to hold the space for his expression, giving full allowance and acceptance, without hijacking his story and making it about us. As a grief counselor, Ted is trained and adept at being a witness. Still, I could see how difficult it could be for the average person to not get involved in the stories of his family and friends. I could feel the impact of such compassionate witnessing. Could it be the greatest gift we can give and the most valuable to receive?

Through the continuous healing process of grief, we tend to the water in our "boats". We avoid the rocky hazards of suppressed wounds and the increased drama and trauma in their wake. Our losses become the new found wisdom that propels us forward. We sail into our present rather than react to our past, and our "boats" are better able to navigate the waves along the way.

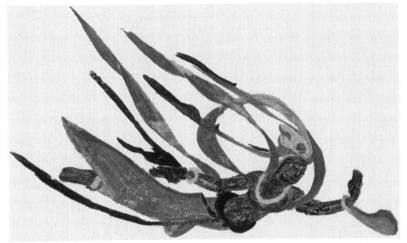

In the midst of heat from loss comes the
opportunity to find our pure essence.

The Wild Turkey

Fall of 1996 - Cairns, Australia

The humid air filled Ted's lungs as he hiked in the ancient rain-forest. Head down, he maneuvered his feet through the large tree roots. He felt small and powerless under the towering canopy. Besieged by green lushness, he took in one damp breath after another.

This long journey had taken him from Hawaii to New Zealand and now to Cairns in Queensland. Australia had been his fantasy escape while Leslie was undergoing chemotherapy. Five years later, he was there, but he walked alone.

It seemed like the perfect escape. In this place, there were no memories of the family he had lost. Here, he was safe from the woeful stares and the hollow platitudes of well-meaning friends. Here, he was buffered from the silence that filled his house, the empty rocker where Leslie breastfed the girls, away from their bedrooms, colorful and happy, yet now sad and empty.

In Australia, he wasn't haunted by the countless remnants of his life, but the anguish remained.

Perhaps it was restlessness that drew him to the 110-million-year-old Daintree National Park. Maybe some answers lurked in its primordial beauty. Perhaps it held some peace for him in some form. Even the jaws of a hungry crocodile seemed a welcome end to this pain.

The wonders of this ancient forest fell away unnoticed with each step, but the sight of the wild turkey crossing his path jolted Ted into the present. A wild turkey in the middle of the rainforest? he thought.

He became aware of the day: Thanksgiving. The knowledge seeped through him as he envisioned his family gathered together. It all goes on whether I am there or not. It all goes on, he thought.

The turkey in his path hinted at a bigger picture, calling him back to home and to healing.

The Importance of Conscious Grieving

The next morning, Ted gave me a tour of Golden Willow Retreat. Although I had visited many times, this tour was to demonstrate how every detail of the retreat was intended to create a sacred space for healing.

We began outside. Surrounded by the Sangre de Cristo Mountains, it seemed as if we were held in the palm of the earth herself.

As we walked toward the entrance, we stopped at a golden willow tree, a gift from Ted's siblings. The retreat had been named for the tree and for its symbolism: gold represented the alchemy of healing.

"In the midst of heat from loss comes the opportunity to find our pure essence," Ted said.

The willow was chosen because of its strength to stand, its ability to bend in the wind, and its capacity (and thus its invitation) to weep.

As we wove our way through the retreat center, I felt a sense of solace and connection through its design as well as its artwork. The community room adjoined the kitchen, creating an open flow. Its many windows looked out on the expanse of the mountains. The well-appointed bedrooms had doors to the outside, reinforcing the idea that visitors could come and go as they wished.

Standing in the doorway of "The Cave" had a great impact on me. As I descended the three steps into the room, it seemed that I was coming down to meet myself. This room was used for counseling and workshops. This was where you could strip off all masks and be vulnerable. Ted and I spent a lot of our time in "The Cave"; his dry erase marker drew out the grief process on the white board, and his teaching conveyed the raw emotion of his own experience.

Early in one of our "cave sessions", Ted elaborated on how we create unnecessary cycles of trauma by suppressing our emotions. I learned that when we suffer a loss that shakes our foundation, we turn inward, enclosing ourselves in a chrysalis of grief. Because a recent loss is infused with all those previous, we revert to the age of our last acknowledged loss. In a society that honors intellect and largely devalues the tools to grieve, the age to which we regress may be quite young.

Stuck in the past and fearful of the future, we are like puppets controlled by the younger emotional self. We are driven by the need to avoid our pain, which lives in the present. We revert to survival habits that no longer work, we gravitate to the generational means of coping that were modeled for us in our youth, and we grab at anything to distract us in an attempt to feel in control and safe.

Our actions defy the logic of our chronological age, further isolating us. We feel alone, sick, scared, and crazy. We close off our heart, cutting ourselves off from others and from our higher power.

In a futile attempt to gain control and achieve a different outcome, we unconsciously attract situations to reenact the losses from our past, but this creates more of the same. We experience the same unsatisfying or even damaging relationships. We marry someone like our abusive father or our aloof mother. We attract others to repeat experiences of abandonment and betrayal. The abused becomes the abuser, the repressed becomes the repressor, and the victim becomes the perpetrator.

Flowing farther from connection to our heart, we become like a fearful child- needy and noisy. Vacillating between bullying and people pleasing, we manipulate or intimidate others in an attempt to get comfortable in our dis-ease. We numb ourselves, falling prey to our addiction of choice: drugs, alcohol, gambling, pornography, shopping, video or computer games, food, sex, television, or work.

When we are ready, an opportunity to engage in healing emerges and we may choose to consciously express our emotions surrounding the loss. Opening up our chrysalis of grief, however slightly, helps to release us from our toxic prison. We connect to our natural emotions through telling and retelling our story. Our feelings are seen, heard, and valued and a connection to our higher power is restored.

Synchronicity, or "God shots" as Ted calls them, are our calls to conscious healing. These seemingly magical or unexplained events awaken us to the present moment and the awareness that there is something greater at work in our lives. In this glimpse of a bigger picture, we reconnect with our spiritual nature, and we realize that it takes just as much energy to remain isolated in a chrysalis as it does to wiggle free.

Through the lifelong grief process, the psyche moves up its emotional timeline to become more current. We have integrity in our choices and actions. Our losses become our facts, not our defining truth. We allow our feelings to guide us and blossom into wisdom. We adopt tools that help us to express our emotions in a healthy manner and to connect even further. Our self-perception evolves to that of our true self, one filled with love, forgiveness, and gratitude.

It's never a straight path to healing and the path has no end. It is, in fact, The Hero's Journey (as originally described by Joseph Campbell) that takes us up the ladder of emotional healing. It allows our true essence- an essence free of lies and manipulation- to shine and to become pure in intent, free of victimhood and co-dependence, to become one of compassion, insight, and grace.

To heal, we must step into our metaphoric cave. We find the courage to go within and to sit exposed and in pain. Again and again, we take these steps down but emerge and are lifted up by our tears. That which seems overwhelming is bearable when experienced one step at a time. The guidance for each step is found in the present.

With no road map and no estimated time of arrival,
we journey with our emotions, one step at a time.

The Shedding

Spring of 1997 - Taos, New Mexico

Ted stopped in his tracks as the large snake reared up and faced him. At first startled, he saw that it was not a diamondback rattler but a harmless bull snake. The snake seemed unpredictable and skittish. It lunged and backtracked at the same time.

Upon inspection, Ted saw why the snake was so defensive. The eyes of its flattened head were a cloudy, bluish white. Its four-foot-long stretch of skin was dull. This snake was preparing to shed. The new skin underneath would be sensitive and easily irritated. Even the breeze would sting.

Half-blind and in discomfort, the snake was fearful of Ted's approach.

Ted turned away, leaving the snake to its process. Soon it would shed. Soon it would display beautiful, shiny skin, and its eyes would be clear.

Ted realized that the snake was a mirror of himself. His own eyes and mind were clouded and dull. He felt out of control, sad in one moment and angry in the next. "If onlys" ran through his mind as if he could rewrite the past.

Blame, guilt, anger, and shame danced through his being and churned in his mind. Was he being punished? How did the collision with the truck happen? It just didn't make sense! How could God do this? What lesson was he not getting?

He wondered who he was under the skin that no longer fit him, the skin that was Leslie's husband, the skin that was the father to Keri and Amy.

This is how the snake grows, he thought, and in that moment, he felt a whisper of hope.

Grief Stew

The tiny coffee shop in the Taos Plaza was bustling. Regulars visited over steaming cups surrounded by stickers on the wall that proclaimed "Be the Change You Want to See in the World" and "Fight Corporate Domination - Your Ignorance Is Their Power."

We left its funky warmth and found a sunny spot in the Plaza. Taos stirred lazily around us in the cool morning air, and the heat from my cup warmed my hands.

Ted was discussing Elisabeth Kubler-Ross's groundbreaking book that was published over forty years ago. The five stages of grief outlined in *On Death and Dying* transformed the subjects of bereavement and death. This model of the grief cycle had been applied globally to therapy and counseling for emotional trauma.

Ted explained that some see the stages as a chronological checklist of the healing process, which was not Ross's intent. In fact, there were no boxes to be checked off and, although the process progressed, it was never complete.

The five well-known stages- *Denial, Anger, Bargaining, Depression, and Acceptance-* are far from linear and therefore Ted referred to them as aspects. In grieving, we find ourselves jumping from one aspect to another and even experiencing more than one aspect at a time.

Ted likened the grief process to a pot full of stew. There are key ingredients, and we may find ourselves taking a bite of one or more in any spoonful. The "stew" is spiced with all the other losses we have experienced that are being stirred up from the bottom of the pot. With conscious "chewing", its nutrients will nourish us, but the pot never empties. We just taste of it less often and its spices are less intense.

Consciously tasting of our "stew" is extremely important. Without conscious healing, the aspects of grief continuously cycle through Denial, Anger, and Bargaining. To avoid painful emotions, we subconsciously close off to the Depression and Acceptance aspects, never stepping down into the heart long enough to connect to a higher power and the alchemy of healing. The losses are left intellectualized and buried. We remain stunted in a regressed emotional state, thereby causing behavior that is incongruent with our true self. The disparity continues until an event happens that demands we become conscious of the wound. The wider the gap, the more drastic the event may be.

When we open up to the aspects of Depression and Acceptance, we allow ourselves to connect to the emotions in our hearts. Vulnerability ushers in true healing, but the psyche will only bear so much before we turn to another aspect while we bolster the strength to face the pain.

Many feel defeated when they feel that their grief is complete and the pain reappears. Instead, this is a testimony to their growth. They are ready to process another piece of the loss, a piece that they could not have processed before, and this leads them to more healing and more self-realization.

Grief is a lifelong process. With no road map or estimated time of arrival, we journey with our emotions one step at a time. With tools that aid conscious expression, we open to our higher wisdom and live more and more in the present than in the wounds of our past.

Ted went into each aspect in depth so that I would better understand how they worked together and how he had experienced them in his own healing. He retained his respect for Kubler-Ross's work but gave the aspects different names. He felt that the alternate names held less of a negative connotation and better honored our natural emotions.

Ted called the aspects Insulation, Protest, Connecting the Dots, Surrender, and Acknowledgement. His model also included a sixth ingredient in the "stew", Relocation. He shared that in this aspect, we experience our personal evolution with renewed purpose and meaning.

In this book, we use the names interchangeably, capitalizing the first letter of the words to honor their importance in the natural healing process.

Possessing no timeline or measuring stick, grief
is unique to each of us and necessitates that
we be patient with our self and others.

The Ponderosa Forest

Summer of 1975 - West of Los Alamos, New Mexico in the Jemez Mountains

The glorious June day was just beginning to cool. The smell of pine permeated the clearing where twelve-year-old Ted and his buddy made camp. Although they were close to home, they imagined that they were on an adventure. Gazing up at the 150-foot-tall ponderosa trees, they envisioned they were far away, free from parents and chores, free to explore and discover.

The boys turned when they heard the crackle of the pine needles. The late afternoon light showed a typical looking Los Alamos government worker, early thirties with a groomed beard, clad in a button-down over a t-shirt, slacks and tennis shoes. It seemed safe to agree to let him camp nearby.

Later, they wandered over to his camp and he offered them whiskey. Soon after, he brought out some girlie magazines. Ted felt uncomfortable, but not wanting to feel left out, he drank some of the whiskey and feigned interest in the magazines.

After a while, the stars seemed to swirl around his head. His speech was slurred, if he even managed to speak at all. The man helped the boys up and over to their sleeping bags that lay open under the dome of the starry night.

Grateful to be lying down but terribly dizzy, Ted recoiled in disgust when he felt the man's penis in his hand. Instinctively, he rolled over to get away. He lay there in the dark, curled in a tense ball and shocked out of his stupor.

What was happening to his friend? The sucking sounds seemed to go on forever. He wrapped himself tighter in his blanket and let his body relax only when he heard the man walk away.

The man left with the sunrise. Ted and his friend looked at each other through eyes forever changed. With one glance, they both knew that they would never discuss what had happened. They would never tell anyone. In the shock and shame, there were no words.

Denial and Insulation

The mountains towered around us as the SUV climbed the road to Taos Ski Valley. These mountains were twice the height of my North Carolina Appalachians, yet these were the adolescents, rugged, growing, and shifting in fits of defiance.

The much older Blue Ridge Mountains of home lost their rugged countenance long ago. Mother Nature had chiseled them with wind and ice and rain until they were fractions of their former selves. They were ancient, and, having experienced it all, more settled.

On the windy switchbacks, Ted taught me about Ganesha. The popular Hindu deity represented by the elephant is widely worshiped and revered as the remover of obstacles.

Ted explained that sometimes Ganesha doesn't remove an obstacle, but instead blocks your path. In this way, he forces you to choose another direction.

In the grief process, Denial is Ganesha blocking our path.

When in Denial, dubbed Insulation by Ted, we are unable to sit with a loss because we lack the emotional infrastructure to be able to face it. We are well aware of the facts, but the brain is unable to fathom or connect to the reality of it.

Insulation is the protective space that allows us to rebuild our foundation until we are ready to confront the wound. Without it, the overload on the psyche would be too much and we would combust emotionally.

Through Denial, we flow in and out of the reality of the loss. Eventually, we are able to ebb closer to the loss until, needing more insulation from the pain, we flow away again. This is the massage of healing that eases us through the many levels of Insulation.

As each loss is stirred and seasoned with the previous losses, time spent in the Insulation aspect may be misunderstood. Efforts to force us into the reality of a loss can be met with resentment, violence, or rage. Possessing no timeline or measuring stick, grief is unique to each person and necessitates that we be patient with our self and others.

Ted warned that it is possible to become firmly rooted in Denial, unable to allow the natural ebb and flow. When unwilling to confront loss, we may self-medicate with our substance of choice, further distorting our natural inclination to heal.

We move farther and farther from the reality until we awaken to healing through another loss, or even the smallest opening of expression to another that enables us to reconnect with the wound and shock us out of our comfortable misery.

Keeping our feet in the present as much as possible is a way to ease closer to the healing process. Because the pain lives in the present moment, we may, at times, be able to accomplish this only through rituals.

Rituals are the drumbeats of our world. They are the practices we have chosen to help us thrive. Rising from bed and feeling our feet connect with the floor is a ritual, as is sipping morning coffee, a weekly lunch with a friend, or attending a church service or Alcoholics Anonymous meeting.

Rituals ground us. We consciously engage in our day-to-day being-ness, if ever so briefly, and thus open ourselves to the present, allowing more connection and more flow to happen.

In Insulation, Ganesha not only blocks us from emotional pain that we aren't ready to face, he helps us to prepare for our journey through rituals.

The expression of protest in a safe environment
as part of our story allows its power to be freed
and harnessed for healthy passions.

The Door to Rage

Ted turned and charged out the door, the slam echoing in his wake. His blood was boiling. Heat wafted off of him as he strode into the sticky day. He had to run out before he did something he would regret. Was he that out of control? Could rage so engulf him that he didn't know who he was anymore?

He could still hear her words taunting him, suggesting that he was responsible for the death of his girls. At first he was stunned. Then he heard a primal scream rise from his throat. He felt his body tense and his fists flail at the air as if he battled unseen demons. He started back toward her but then fled, fearful of what he felt.

She knew his pain, and yet she seemed to want to hurt him. How could she have said that to him? Had he murdered his kids? Was it his fault for coaching that day? His mind churned and his rage boiled.

He was like a simmering pot of anger most of the time. He was angry with himself, angry with Leslie's cancer, angry with the truck that took the girls' lives. He was angry with God for punishing him and angry that he couldn't understand the lesson he should be getting. What was he missing?

At least when they argued, he felt alive. He felt the blood rush to his face and could feel himself in his body. The relationship helped him that way. No matter that his heart was closed off and she would never be Leslie. No matter that he felt sick and dead and crazy and alone. Maybe she could rescue him after all.

Anger and Protest

Ted and Marcella's dogs, Jasmine and Bella, accompanied me on my jog. Our breath was visible on the frosty morning air. Jasmine proudly took the lead while Bella trailed behind, running on three legs to protect the bandaged one.

A few weeks prior, Bella had attempted an escape from the courtyard. She climbed on the back of a chair and took a mighty leap, her back leg catching in the scrollwork at the top of the gate. For several moments, she hung there, and although she cried for help, it was Jasmine's screams that caught Marcella's attention.

Ted recalled that day and Jasmine's intense but normal reaction. Seeing her sibling in distress registered throughout her body. She howled and shook all over, as if having a seizure. Her reaction was instant and uninhibited.

The human brain not only allows the inhibition of emotions, it may prefer it. The brain's reaction to any event is to shuffle through the files of the past so that it can predict a future outcome. Unlike animals, the human brain is focused everywhere *but* in the present.

Additionally, humans have been conditioned to believe that expressing emotion, particularly Anger, is to be weak. Add to that self-consciousness, and we can understand why we mask emotions to appear in control, which brings us a semblance of safety.

In truth, Anger is a natural response to losing something of value that has been ripped from us. We tend to look at Anger as a negative, but it is as valuable an emotion as joy, excitement, and giddiness. It is only the behavior that expresses the emotion that may be deemed positive or negative.

Protest, as Ted calls it, allows us to give voice to frustrations surrounding a loss. It serves as an escape valve, allowing us to express our pain over a shattered reality.

Protest is often our first attempt to be present instead of locked in the past and fearful of the future. It can be the spark that jumpstarts a numbed heart.

Anger can lead us to Denial as we weave through the healing process. We Protest the loss and assign blame. We Protest that we are not in control of what is being written in our lives. We feel angry when we hear well-meaning platitudes like "God needed her more than we did" or "everything happens for a reason," particularly if we don't feel that way. When the harsh reality of a loss is forced upon us before our emotional infrastructure is ready, we may experience rage before we move toward Denial for more insulation.

Protest may be expressed in irrational ways. We may displace it and lash out at someone who is trying to help when we are actually angry at being abandoned by the death of a loved one. When we take steps to consciously name the source of the Anger, we engage in healthy Protest and are doing the work to heal.

Likewise, if we repress our natural impulses of Protest, healthy Anger may turn toxic. Unclaimed Anger leads to resentment, which may escalate to rage or silent, verbal, or physical attacks on others, self, or things. New problems and sources of grief are created, causing us to further isolate and numb ourselves with addictions.

Conscious Protest is part of the personal power that we integrate into our true identity through the healing process. The expression of Protest in a safe environment as part of our story allows its power to be freed and harnessed for healthy passions.

When interacting with loved ones in the grief and loss process, it's important to be nonjudgmental and even detached, within healthy boundaries, when they express Anger. Like the snake shedding its skin, they are in discomfort and will strike at those close to them. Eventually, their eyes will open to the true source of their pain.

From the beginning of time, the brain has
been driven to connect the dots.

Capsized

Spring of 1989 - Taos, New Mexico

It had been only days now since Ted heard about Richard. Most of the family had gathered at his mom and Charlie's house, praying that Richard would be found alive. After what seemed like an eternity, Ted's brother Rob called to confirm that the only body recovered from the capsized boat in the freezing Alaskan waters was indeed their brother's.

"Dammit!" Ted screamed as the hammer made contact with his thumb. He tried to be productive by remodeling Leslie's and his house, but his mind kept churning on Richard's death. Leslie gave him a wide berth. She had loved Richard too, but Ted felt alone in this loss, much like he guessed she had when she miscarried a few years prior.

He was mad at himself, mad that once, when Richard was three years old, he made Richard cry by telling him they would all die one day. Now Richard was dead. He relived the shame that he had felt that day. If only he could take those words back!

Rob got him into commercial fishing, Ted thought. Rob should have looked after Richard and not made him join a different crew just because of a slight mishap the summer before. If Richard had sailed with Rob like he always had, he would still be here. If only Richard hadn't been on that boat.

The Exxon Valdez was really to blame. The spill of millions of gallons of oil caused The Legend to scout out another route through the Aleutians for salmon. The original route was far from the storm. The Legend never should have been there. It never should have capsized. Richard should be alive!

What about Janice? If she hadn't died of a heart defect, Richard wouldn't have gotten into commercial fishing in the first place. He would have spent his summers with his girlfriend- hell, she would probably be his wife by now. If Janice had lived, Richard would be here too.

Why is this happening? How could my baby brother die before me? This never should have happened! So many things could have happened differently to prevent this. God, I could have been a better brother. He was mine to take care of.

In his heart, Ted carried the blame.

Bargaining and Connecting the Dots

I awoke before dawn and caught Ted in the kitchen before his first appointment arrived. For the last two nights, my dreams had been particularly vivid. In the latest one, I was riding in a minivan that wrecked in a ditch. Then, I was on a foot-powered scooter and stopped to save an owlet from a circling hawk. I cradled the owlet close to me as the hawk trailed us. The frightened bird bit me, leaving a diamond-shaped wound at the center of my throat. With the hawk no longer in sight, I held the baby further from me and soon came upon a larger owlet. I sensed the mother was close by and left the bird there.

Ted listened patiently to the dream and acknowledged that by listening to his story, I had been given permission to go to mine. In my dreamtime, I was mining wisdom from my past.

I was revisiting the loss of my job ten months earlier, my inability to speak my truth and have balance in that position, and the recent birth of my coaching career that offered me both.

The brain is driven to connect the dots. In early civilizations, humans gazed at the night sky, and, trying to make sense of their place in the vastness, found in the stars images and mythologies that gave them purpose, safety, and a sense of control.

Ted explained that in grief, the brain strives to Connect the Dots to make sense of the loss. It continually processes the events of the past in an attempt to make the future more predictable and thus safer. The Bargaining aspect is the brain's debate with the illusion of control.

In this illusion, we are much like the director of our own life movie watching scenes that we didn't write or call for. We want to rewind and reshoot to keep it from being real, but of course, that is impossible.

We attempt to reclaim the loss through negotiation. The brain spins with thoughts of "If only-"," but how-", "I could have-", and "this shouldn't have-". We hear the mind's "monkey chatter" and the shoulda, coulda, wouldas as it processes the loss.

Bargaining is a natural expression of grief and, although painful, it needs to be allowed to run its course. We bear compassionate witness to self or loved ones as the mind spins and searches, trying to work things out.

In this aspect, we may get lost in the wilderness of guilt and shame. As the "director" of our movie, we take the blame for not having protected that character or that scene. When sharing these feelings of personal responsibility, we may be judged by others as irrational, which reinforces the belief that we are crazy or wrong. Still others may shower us with reassurances that become addictive and keep us in a self-defeating cycle.

Eventually, the brain finds a way to Connect the Dots. It doesn't matter if the connection is grounded in reality or that it makes sense to anyone but the griever. The brain has found a way to make peace with the wound and the loss of control. Reality begins to set in.

Along with Denial and Anger, Bargaining is a natural impulse to protect ourselves as we heal. The jagged rocks of grief are dulled as we progress toward healing. We build up our capacity to face what is in our heart. Our stamina to touch the reality of loss increases over time as we move toward Acceptance.

When all of our efforts to avoid the pain of our reality fail, when our debate with the illusion of control in bargaining is exhausted, when denial is no longer working, we surrender to profound sorrow.

The Choice

Summer of 1996 - Albuquerque, New Mexico

Ted sat helpless and aware that the choice was Keri's now. It was up to Keri to choose if her soul would remain in her shattered body or move on.

Could it have been only that morning that Ted got Charlie's call? "Ted, this is not a joke" Charlie had said. "The girls have been in a bad car crash with Rachel. Amy and Rachel didn't make it, and it looks bad for Keri- very bad."

After a surgery in Taos, Keri's broken body was transferred by helicopter to a hospital in Albuquerque. Recalling his long days in this very hospital with Leslie, Ted now gazed at their daughter, a jigsaw of swelling and tubes. He felt utterly powerless.

He told her that he loved her and that if she wanted to heal and stay with him, he would support her with anything she needed. If she needed to go with sissy and mommy, that was okay. She didn't need to stay here to look after him. He would be alright.

The words echoed in his ears. Would he really be alright? He had to let her think so.

He held her left hand just as he did when he drove her to school. Though exhausted and profoundly sad, he was determined to stay strong for her. He spoke of their fond memories and let her know how much she was loved.

Keri's brain started to hemorrhage and, with the choice made, her soul continued on its path.

Depression and Surrender

Ted ran toward the window in disbelief. He glimpsed something large, a coyote or a wolf, running just outside the Golden Willow courtyard toward the mountains. The thing in its jaws appeared to be a cat. Not used to seeing these predators so close, he made sure that Bella and Jasmine were secure, knowing that they might give chase.

I felt as if the circle of life had just played out before my eyes and was reminded how far I was from the city. I said a silent blessing for the cat who gave its life so that another animal would be nourished and then one for the cat's owners who would soon feel its loss.

We returned to our lesson on Depression. Ted reinforced that in this context, the word referred not to a clinical depression, although it could lead to that, but rather to deep sadness. When all efforts to avoid the pain of our reality fail, when our debate with the illusion of control in Bargaining is exhausted, when Denial is no longer working, we Surrender to profound sorrow.

We Surrender to knowing that we do not write or direct our movie. We Surrender the belief that we have control over the path of others. Everything we thought we knew about the way things should be falls away and leaves us feeling sorrowful and empty.

The Surrender aspect is one of great vulnerability and stark aloneness. We feel powerless. None of the tools we used to manage our world are working. We Surrender our struggle to stay on the surface of the loss and sink into the well of grief. We connect with the emotions in our heart, naked, exhausted, and in pain. It is the journey of the dark night of the soul, a journey that we all must traverse alone.

Though Surrender is fraught with heart-wrenching sorrow, it is the path of true healing. We have built an infrastructure sufficient to scaffold down into the empty abyss and confront our wound. Our frostbitten heart begins to painfully thaw to life.

We pick up the tools that help us express what we are feeling. We open to our spirituality, we write grief letters, we share our story, we journal, we paint, or we sit in meditation, allowing tears to dampen our cheeks.

This journey to the abyss is not the end. When the pain becomes too difficult to bear, we return to the surface to gain more emotional infrastructure. We return to Denial, Anger, and Bargaining again and again in our dance with healing, growing ever stronger, so that we may Surrender again to grief.

There is no timeline for how long we might stay in this aspect before entering another and it can be difficult to watch our loved ones in deep sorrow. We want to help them, but we are at the mercy of their healing process. By patiently holding the space that allows them to experience their pain, we help them to heal. We must claim this space for ourselves as well and have faith that it is necessary to the journey. In the midst of shattering, we must hold ourselves.

The vulnerability of Surrender is the elevator that leads up toward Acceptance. It is the necessary path of reconnecting with the reality of the loss and knowing that we are in a natural healing process.

Just as the seeds of the new are in the shell of the old, we don't discard our past; it is where we glean wisdom to step forward more consciously.

Taos Mountain

Winter of 1976 - Taos Ski Valley, New Mexico

Ted surveyed the area from the top of the ridge. Maybe Taos wasn't all that bad. He did great on the ski team and liked working with his tennis coach.

He never thought he'd like it, but he never thought he'd be ok with his mom and Charlie Anderson getting married either. He stood there remembering the day his life turned upside down five years earlier.

He was eight years old and had heard the word "divorce" just a few weeks before when their neighbors, the Andersons, said they were getting one. Ted remembered joking with his cousin Tami, "What if Dr. Anderson marries my mom and Dad marries Mrs. Anderson?"

There was no laughter as his parents sat their five children down to break the news. His world seemed to blur, and he couldn't sense where he started and his brothers and sister stopped. He fought back tears. Was it his fault? If only he hadn't made that joke to Tami, maybe his dad wouldn't have moved out.

He knew he was to blame when his mom announced that she was marrying Dr. Anderson. For months, Ted protested the marriage by calling him "Sergeant" instead of Charlie- he would never call him "dad."

Things seemed to settle down until his mom and the Sergeant said the family was leaving Los Alamos for a new beginning in

Taos. Ted felt that the move was punishment for causing his parents' divorce. He didn't need a new beginning. He needed his friends in Los Alamos.

He hated Taos the minute he saw it. Through his resentful eyes, it seemed little more than a one-road town with a Plaza where they sold cheap Indian souvenirs. Everything seemed dried up, dead, and sad. He despised the old adobe house they moved into and hated that he was now a minority who was teased for his light hair and ruddy coloring.

Last summer at the commune, things changed. He was amazed that his mom let him go, even if it was friends of hers that ran it. It was fantastic! He loved sharing food, music, families, and life with the other members. He loved learning about different spiritual practices like meditation, guided imagery, and Buddhism. He especially loved walking with the unclothed women to the hot springs.

After that, Taos seemed different. He saw the beautiful mountains that surrounded him and felt comforted, as if they held him. He could appreciate the creativity of the artists in the town and now counted the Native American and Hispanic kids as his friends. Mostly, he liked the skiing.

Maybe, at thirteen, he was getting wiser.

He laughed to himself and pushed off from the ridge, the edges of his skis cutting into the dry, white powder. He carved into the snow, leaving lines behind and, like an artist with a brush, painted his way down the mountain.

Acceptance and Acknowledgment

We parked the car and walked up the gravel incline. The air was fresh and it felt good to stretch my legs. Snow was late coming to Taos Ski Valley and sparse remnants of an earlier fall were protected in the shade.

This was the path that Ted had walked with Leslie and then, the girls. It led to their favorite picnic spot in the meadow. He shared stories about them as we climbed, and I told him about my experience with my father's passing seven years ago.

As we topped the hill, I took in the expanse. It was beautiful: the mountains in the distance nestled between blue sky and grassy carpet, and now, it was one of the resting places for the ashes of his loved ones.

Marcella had given him a small, ceramic cat figurine; he pulled it from his pocket. The ashes of their cat, Layla, were spread here too. He placed it tenderly on the ground amid the figures of angels that adorned the girls' memorial site.

Ted walked toward the meadow as I sat by the memorial, connecting to those it commemorated. In the stillness of my heart, I heard a voice say, *Write our story*. Tears spilled from my eyes as I silently asked, Who are you? The reply was instant: *We are one*.

This truth settled in my being. I rose to join Ted and, with one last glance at the vista, we walked back down the narrow trail.

When we are able to sit in our heart and connect with our pain, something magical happens. Acceptance is the alchemy that transforms the lead of our sorrow into the fuel that propels us forward. We connect to hope and to the possibilities of continuing on our life path. We give birth to a new perception of self, one that is not defined by the loss, but is wiser because of it.

The word "Acceptance" does not mean that we have reached a point where the loss is okay. It may never be okay. Instead, we are able to Acknowledge the loss objectively; it is an event on our timeline and not a definition of who we are.

Acceptance also doesn't mean that we suddenly forgive those associated with the loss or become blind to the error of an action. We continue doing the work of conscious grieving and, in so doing, progress toward our true essence. Along the way, we may find the grace of forgiveness which further opens us to healing.

On the path of healing, we find the space to lovingly touch what is lost through our memories. Just as the seeds of the new are in the shell of the old, we don't discard our past. It is where we glean wisdom to step forward more consciously. It is how we nourish growth and transition back into life.

As we heal and become more self-realized, the journey continues. Pain will rise to the surface again, proving our growth and our infrastructure's ability to face more. We may again try to flee the pain before we Surrender to our well of sorrow, but we can use the tools that we have acquired to consciously climb back up the ladder to Acceptance. We encounter the other aspects, but the frequency, intensity, and duration of the pain lessen.

Through expressing and honoring our loss, we are reborn into a new life.

Our love for what is lost is integrated and we relocate or transfer that love through us in a more expansive way.

Capallita de las Angelitas (Chapel of Angels)

Spring of 2003 - Golden Willow Retreat, Arroyo Hondo, New Mexico

Every piece of this chapel stood for something. Ted looked on in satisfaction as his students finished the building. They planned to hold the blessing ceremony the next evening.

The group of children, aged eleven to thirteen, drew the blueprints and participated in every part of the project. They found creative ways to integrate meaning into this sacred space.

Made possible by the education fund given to Keri and Amy by the community when Leslie died, the vision for the chapel was to welcome everyone. Always open and heated during the winter, it was free of rules and not exclusive to any religion.

The chapel measured fourteen feet and three inches wide as a tribute to Simon. Simon came to live with Ted and Leslie at a turbulent time when he was fourteen years and three months old. Leslie was like a mother to him and the girls were like his sisters. Because he wasn't a blood relative, Simon's grief was largely dismissed by the community, as well as by himself. The width of the chapel paid honor to all of the disenfranchised grievers who feel their story doesn't matter.

The girls died in 1996. The significance of the last two digits was not lost on Ted; the top plate, or bond beam, measured 9 feet long. Keri was nine when she died. The bottom edge of the cross to the top of the roof measured 6 feet for Amy, who was six.

The cross facing the sunset was for Leslie, who possessed a calming, grounded essence. The opposite cross, facing the sunrise, was for Richard, who was always eager to take on the newness of the day.

At the winter and summer solstices, the sun rose through the glass panes of one cross and set through the panes of the other.

Some belongings of Richard, Leslie, Keri, and Amy were buried under the floorboards in the middle of the chapel, symbolically transforming the physical to the metaphysical.

Each student had a special space in the chapel that was sacred. Two boys placed their father's ashes under the floorboards near the altar so that they could "stand" with their father if they later married there.

One boy built the hearth for the grandfather who had added much richness and warmth to his family's lives.

Another boy used his father's tools to build the chapel. His father was lost in drug addiction, but his tools helped to add something good to the world.

The boys all took turns carving alcoves in the walls.

The ceiling was vaulted so that the visitors' feelings and prayers could rise.

The building efforts began on Thanksgiving, signifying the healing that happens when gratitude pours in.

The chapel contained 4,320 adobe bricks, and each one was blessed by the boys and members of the Taos community.

The blessing ceremony was set for Easter, a day that symbolizes rebirth. As the earth awakened from its wintery nap, it would seem as if all of nature was celebrating.

Relocation

"Red is for the healing path, purple is for introspection, yellow is for new beginnings, white is for wisdom, and blue is for abundance," Ted explained. Perhaps sensing that I needed some time alone, he walked out the chapel door. I picked up a yellow candle and moved toward the altar.

It was a season of new beginnings for me. In less than a year, I had a new career, a new sense of balance and identity, a new way of being in the world, and the beginning of my life without my beloved dog of sixteen years, Ace.

Tears filled my eyes as I thought of him. They fill my eyes still. As a witness to much of my pain and growth, as a constant companion to me, the compact Jack Russell Terrier embodied joy. His unconditional love strengthened my sense of self-worth. Six months after his death, I still missed him beyond belief.

I chose the perfect spot among the other candles and cherished articles that signified something greater and lit the wooden match. The wick caught quickly. I closed my eyes and offered my prayer.

"I light this candle in honor of all that I have learned, all that I have been, all that I have released, all that I have healed, and for how I will use this wisdom in my service to others."

I watched as the flame danced on the wick and, feeling it was complete, turned and stepped through the chapel door into the bright sunny day. Ted greeted me with a smile.

Ted's sixth aspect, Relocation, takes us from merely surviving a loss to thriving. We transform the physical loss to the meta-physical, stepping fully into the present and connected to our higher power. Our love for what is lost is integrated and we Relocate or transfer that love in a more expansive way.

On our path to Relocation, we encounter forgiveness, faith, gratitude, love, and healing. We are able to embrace the gift of what our loss gave us before it disappeared. Our hearts become open and full. We are at peace with life as it unfolds and we are fully aware of our ability to heal and evolve further.

In the Relocation of our love, we commemorate the loss. We may create or participate in ceremonies that offer us a con-tainer for our most sacred feelings. We might light a candle for our loved one, build a shrine at an accident site, form a charita-ble foundation, or create an artistic tribute. Our expression of relocating our acknowledged losses to that which transcends them might be outwardly visible or completely private; they may be done with those of like mind or alone.

In fully releasing our losses to our higher power, we reclaim and harness that love for meteoric growth. The Hero emerges, ready to step into the path of service with the resurrection of wisdom and healing.

We know that there will be more suffering on our path but we are full of hope; we trust our spiritual connection for guidance.

We consciously choose to embrace life fully and are at peace with its beautiful fragility.

With an open heart and the integrated power and wisdom of our losses, we fly to our true essence with new purpose and meaning.

© Jerry N. Uelsmann

We use our tools to climb out of the abyss and up
the ladder to acceptance, and from
that ladder, we learn to soar.

The Crooked Path

Fall of 2010 - Taos Ski Valley, New Mexico

Ted dropped off his last grief client of the day. Fatherless, thirteen-year-old Hector lived in Taos Pueblo. They had spent their time together today eating ice cream. Ted liked to meet with kids outside of the counseling office; they seemed more relaxed and open.

He started toward Golden Willow Retreat, but surprised himself by taking the road to Taos Ski Valley. Ted followed the winding road, then parked and continued on foot.

Soon, he reached the meadow. It was a clear, crisp day and the sun was nearly behind the ridge. Patches of icy snow dotted the shadows.

What great picnics they had here, first as a family and then later with just the girls. He smiled as he recalled their little arms and legs scissoring away, making snow angels for their mom-angel and filling the valley with laughter.

Their small memorial was at the left. At the foot of the angel figurine laid a heart-shaped rock the girls had placed there for Leslie. Some of their ashes were there. All three of his girls were together.

He sat there a moment, clearing debris and tending the memorial. He looked up, seeing in the distance the ski run that Keri had mastered the season before her death. She had been triumphant and beaming with pride at her accomplishment.

As he stood there, he felt a peace and a sense of gratitude, not only for the wonderful memories he would always have, but for the moments when he felt them near, guiding him.

Spontaneously, he lay down on a patch of the cold whiteness. His arms and legs worked hard against the icy snow. There, that's got it, he thought as he rose. He turned to survey his snow angel and swore that he could hear girlish giggles floating on the breeze.

In the car, he cranked the heater to full blast as he made his way through Valdez. His hands stung and he looked down to see small cuts made by the ice. The cottonwoods glimmered gold with the last hints of sunlight. He gazed at their beauty and smiled, thinking back to the day that he married Marcella in that valley a decade earlier.

He made his way toward home and Golden Willow Retreat.

The Witness

It was our last day together and I still hadn't told him. I was surprised at both my gnawing need and my reluctance. After all, it had been years since I embarked on its healing. I had cried in anguish, touched immense anger, struggled with the shame and brought it into the light. I had spent hours alone, connected to my heart in meditation. Journals chronicled my path of healing. I had entered forgiveness and seen it as a gift for my evolution and service. Why was it coming up now?

I looked out the window to a gorgeous sunrise that framed the mountains and illuminated the chapel in lavenders, oranges, pinks, and yellows. I threw on some clothes and let my camera play in the early morning light, capturing the sunrise and its metaphor of renewed purpose.

We had breakfast and talked in "The Cave", wrapping up our lessons and discussing the book. I knew it was time to share the story with him. I knew that in the safe confines of Golden Willow Retreat, a place where I had connected with Ted to witness his story, it was important to now honor this piece of my own story.

I turned to Ted and, voice shaking, told him that although some of the grief language was new to me, I understood this process because I had been through it. Feeling nearly detached from my body, I shared that as a child, I had been sexually abused. I heard myself connect the dots of my story for him as a solitary tear rolled down my cheek and off my chin.

Ted listened and when I was through, he simply said, "And it was not your fault."

"No, it wasn't," I avowed.

He stood and walked to a picture on the wall. Pointing to it, he added, "And you have learned to use your tools to climb out of the abyss and up the ladder to acceptance." His excitement building, he added, "and from that ladder, you learn to soar."

I nodded, and we shared a silent moment. I was aware, now more than ever, of how healing from loss is never complete, even when it seems it should be. I asked Ted to clarify this last piece for me.

He told me that grief is like an amputation. Something dear has been cut away from us, and even though we do the work to heal the wound, we still need to care for the space between our soul and the scar. Emotions bubble up and may cause blisters in this space. This signifies that we are ready to heal more. Over time, the scar reminds us more of our wisdom than of the wound.

The choice to consciously heal is a wonderful dance that we do throughout life. We work with facing the reality of loss and, in so doing, engage all of our losses. When we find the pain of this reality too much to bear, we dance in and out, sinking into the abyss of our grief and healing as we are able. The dance moves us from numbness to anguish to pain. It takes us through longing, sadness, missing, and gratitude, again and again.

Eventually and consciously, we adjust to the loss and emerge with new direction. We accept and mature emotionally. We forge new relationships and beginnings. We spend more time on the living than on the loss, more time in the present than in the past, and we are rewarded with growth that ushers us forward with renewed intensity and purpose.

When more emotion begs expression, as it will, we know what to do. We know the way up and down the ladder to our well of grief. We honor and express our emotions to a counselor or to another person that we can trust, as well as to ourselves. We claim our vulnerability through journaling, meditation, writing poetry, music or other types of expression.

Our emotional self becomes more congruent with our true self, thereby creating integrity of intent and actions, which fuels our potential. With this integrity comes a calming faith. We claim the connection to our higher power and recognize the divine through our path within.

As we consciously dance through life's healing process, we invite others to do the same. It is hard to watch those that we love suffer, but the greatest gift we can give them is the space to hold their grief. We patiently and compassionately witness and allow their expression, releasing the need to "fix it" or make it about us.

When we hold the space for others to heal, we heal ourselves.

Through grief, we open to our truth. We travel the winding path of reclaiming our self with more authenticity and awareness. There is no direct route and we won't be able to predict where we are headed, but the path is revealed in each breath. The path unfolds with each step, and all is made known to us in the present.

I encourage you to be the witness. Be patient. Be kind. Be compassionate. Most importantly, be all of this for yourself as you progress on the journey to the highest expression of self, one step at a time.

Acknowledgements

Thanks to my husband, Mike, for his love and support, and to the many strong female friends I am graced with on this earth, especially Marcella Wiard and Patricia Young for their decades of witnessing and encouragement. A special thanks to my spiritual coach, Carmen Radson, for her guidance on my path of healing and to Ted Wiard. Without you, Ted, this book would not be possible.

Carol

I want to thank my wife, Marcella for suggesting Carol as the voice for this book. I am also grateful for her ongoing support of my pursuit and wish for conscious healing for All. Thanks to my entire family, my daughter Sophia, and the community which has been inspirational in witnessing, supporting, and honoring my healing path. With special thanks to my angels: Keri, Amy, Richard, and Leslie.

Ted

We also thank Golden Willow Retreat and its board of directors for helping to sponsor this project. A special thanks to John M. Scanlan for his generous contribution of most of the photographs in this book.

About Carol and Ted

Carol Poteat is a writer, speaker, and owner of Partners in Potential, a service-based company that offers personal and business coaching, consulting, and sales training. Her twenty years of experience in advertising sales and management, coupled with her lifelong spiritual journey, have given her the ability to relate to people from all walks of life. Carol lives in Charlotte, North Carolina with her husband, Mike, and enjoys weekend trips to the mountains, golf, and hiking.

To contact Carol or sign up for her newsletter, visit www. PartnersInPotential.com

Ted Wiard, LPCC, CGC, is a licensed clinical therapist, a certified grief counselor, and an ordained minister. He also holds certifications as a schoolteacher and a tennis coaching professional. His passion for working with grief arose from his own personal losses in which he realized there were very few places to go for support. Ted and his wife, Marcella, are the founders of Golden Willow Retreat, an emotional healing center focused on grief, loss, and resiliency located outside of Taos in Arroyo Hondo, New Mexico. Director of Golden Willow Retreat, Ted is also the Clinical Supervisor for TeamBuilders Counseling Services in Taos, which works with children and their families in need of mental health services and community support throughout New Mexico. Ted is sought after for speaking engagements internationally. He has written many articles on the subject of emotional healing and has collaborated with many treatment centers around the country focusing on grief, loss, and the connection-disconnection of spirituality, addiction, and relapse. Ted and Marcella reside in Arroyo Hondo and Santa Fe, New Mexico.

To contact Ted or for more information on Golden Willow Retreat, visit www.GoldenWillowRetreat.org